Sir John Suckling

Shearsman Classics Vol. XXV

Other titles in the *Shearsman Classics* series:

1. *Poets of Devon and Cornwall, from Barclay to Coleridge* (2007)
2. Robert Herrick *Selected Poems* (2007)
3. *Spanish Poetry of the Golden Age, in contemporary English translations* (2008)
4. Mary, Lady Chudleigh *Selected Poems* (2009)
5. William Strode *Selected Poems* (2009)
6. Sir Thomas Wyatt *Selected Poems* (2010)
7. *Tottel's Miscellany* (1557)   (The Tudor Miscellanies, Vol. 1) (2010)
8. *The Phœnix Nest* (1593)   (The Tudor Miscellanies, Vol. 2) (2010)
9. *Englands Helicon* (1600)   (The Tudor Miscellanies, Vol. 3) (2010)
10. Mary Coleridge *Selected Poems* (2010)
11. D.H. Lawrence *Look! We Have Come Through!* (2011)
12. D.H. Lawrence *Birds, Beasts and Flowers* (2011)
13. D.H. Lawrence *Studies in Classic American Literature* (2011)
14. Johann Wolfgang von Goethe *Faust* (translated by Mike Smith) (2012)
15. Robert Browning *Dramatic Romances* (2012)
16. Robert Browning *Sordello* (2012)
17. Robert Browning *The Ring and the Book* (2012)
18. Fernando de Herrera *Selected Poems*
    (translated by Luis Ingelmo & Michael Smith) (2014)
19. Thomas Gray *The English Poems* (2014)
20. Antonio Machado *Solitudes & Other Early Poems*
    (translated by Michael Smith & Luis Ingelmo) (2015)
21. John Donne *Poems (1633)* (2015)
22. Thomas Carew *Collected Poems* (2015)
23. Gerard Manley Hopkins *The Wreck of the Deutschland* (ed. Nigel Foxell) (2017)
24. Gérard de Nerval *Les Chimères* (translated by Will Stone) (2017)
25. Sir John Suckling *Collected Poems* (2020)
26. Richard Lovelace *Collected Poems* (2020)
27. Robert Herrick *Hesperides (1648)* (2018)
28. Algernon Charles Swinburne *Our Lady of Pain: Poems of Eros and Perversion*
    (edited by Mark Scroggins) (2019)
29. Luís de Camões *The Lusiads* (translated by Sir Richard Fanshawe, 1666) (2020)
30. Luís de Camões *Selected Shorter Poems* (translated by Jonathan Griffin) (2020)

The Collected Poems

of

Sir John Suckling

Shearsman Books

First published in the United Kingdom in 2020 by
Shearsman Books Ltd
PO Box 4239
Swindon
SN3 9FN

Shearsman Books Ltd Registered Office
30–31 St. James Place, Mangotsfield, Bristol BS16 9JB
(this address not for correspondence)

www.shearsman.com

Shearsman Classics Vol. 25

ISBN 978-1-84861-612-7

Notes and editorial matter
copyright © Shearsman Books Ltd, 2020

Contents

Introduction	7
His Dream	11
A Supplement of an imperfect Copy of Verses of Mr Will. Shakespear, By the Author	12
Love's Representation	13
[A Barley-break]	15
A Candle	16
A Pedler of Small-Wares	17
A Soldier	18
A Barber	19
Perjury [disdain'd]	20
Loves World	21
The Metamorphosis	24
To B. C.	24
Lutea Allison: Si sola es, nulla es	25
Upon the first sight of my Lady Seimor	26
Non est mortale quod opto : Upon Mrs A. L.	26
Upon A. M.	27
Upon Sir John Laurence's bringing Water over the hills to my Lord Middlesex his House at Wiston	27
A Prologue of the Author's to a Masque at Wiston	28
To my Lady E. C. at her going out of England	29
A Song to a Lute	30
Upon my Lady Carliles walking in Hampton-Court garden	31
Upon T. C. having the P.	32
Love's Burning-glass	33
The Miracle	34
The deformed Mistress	35
Upon L[ady] M[iddlesex] Weeping	36
Detraction Execrated	37
On King Richard the third, who lies buried under Leicester bridge	38
Against Fruition [I]	39
Against Fruition [II]	40
To Mr Davenant for Absence	41
Against Absence	42

[To his Rival 1]	43
To his Rival [II]	44
To a Lady that forbidd to love before Company	46
The Invocation	47
The Expostulation [I]	48
[The Expostulation II]	49
Sonnet I	50
Sonnet II	51
Sonnet III	52
[Love's Sanctuary]	54
[Loves Feast]	55
[Loves Offence]	56
[Desdain]	57
[Disdain] *Englished by the Author*	58
Profer'd Love rejected	59
[The constant Lover]	60
[The Answer]	61
The careless Lover	62
Song	63
Loving and Beloved	65
[Womans Constancy]	66
[Loves Clock]	67
[Song: 65. "No, no, faire heretique"]	68
[Song 66. "Why so pale and wan fond Lover?"]	69
[Loves Siege]	70
Farewel to Love	72
Upon Two Sisters	74
[A Summons to Town]	75
[The Wits] (A Sessions of the Poets)	77
To his much honoured the Lord Lepington, upon his translation of Malvezzi, his 'Romulus' and 'Tarquin'	82
To my Friend Will. Davenant upon his Poem of *Madagascar*	84
(To my Friend Will. Davenant,) On his other Poems	84
An Answer to some Verses made in his Praise	85
A Ballade Upon a Wedding	86
On New-Years Day 1640, To the King	91
Upon my Lord Brohall's Wedding	93

Juvenilia and Seasonal Works

Upon St. Thomas his unbeliefe	95
Upon Christmas Eve	95
Upon Christ his birth	95
Upon Stephen stoned	96
Upon St Johns-day comeing after Christmas day	96
Upon Innocents day	96
Upon Newyeares day	97
Upon the Epiphanie, Or starr that appear'd to the wisemen	97
Upon Christmas	97
[Faith and Doubt]	98
A Dreame	99
Explanatory Notes	100

Introduction

Sir John Suckling (1609–1641) was a significant figure in the group of poets who followed Ben Jonson (often referred to collectively as the "tribe of Ben"), and was a close friend of several others on the group, such as Herrick, Lovelace and Carew. These poets tend to be described as *Cavalier poets*, having been supporters of King Charles I in the English Civil War and, in some cases, having fought actively with the royalist forces. Suckling raised troops and led them into battle – singularly unsuccessfully: it seems they all ran away at the first sign of violence and thus Suckling could proudly report that not one person under his command had been lost in battle. He had a sense of humour, as did many of his friends in the "Tribe". Suckling was also a "wit" – an educated man about town, able to turn a courteous and amusing phrase, or a poetic tribute, but also a gambler, a womaniser, and a man who dabbled in court politics. A card-player of some reputation, he is reputed have invented the game of cribbage.

Not a *great* poet, but still a very good one, Suckling's work can stand alongside that of many of his contemporaries, such as Waller, even if this editor does not rate it as highly as that of, say, Herrick or Carew, not to mention older poets such as Jonson and Donne, whose work is considerably superior. However, it is one of the joys of this period in English letters that there were a number of fine poets of the second rank, who deserve their day in the sun, free from the overwhelming shadows projected by Marlowe, Shakespeare, Jonson, Donne, and – later – Marvell and Milton, two poets whose politics took them into the Parliamentary camp.

John Suckling was the son of a government official who was knighted for his service by King James I in 1616. His father, also John, served as a member of the Privy Council until his death in 1627, and had previously been an MP. John's mother came of a London mercantile family and died in 1613. Young John was born in Twickenham, was educated privately, end entered Trinity College, Cambridge, in 1623. He was later to spend time at Gray's Inn, one of the Inns of Court, not as a trainee lawyer, but – like many a young man of high station – getting some postgraduate training, some of which may well have included matters juridical. He left Gray's Inn upon the death of his father, when he inherited a considerable fortune. He subsequently spent some time with Sir Edward Cecil's forces in the Netherlands, and briefly attended the University of Leiden. He was back in England in 1630, the year he was knighted.

His early life as a knight of the realm was chiefly notable for his louche and spendthrift ways, and his less-than-gallant treatment of certain ladies. His pursuit of Anne Willoughby, perhaps for pecuniary reasons in the wake of his own excess spending, was rejected by her father, and – given a number of other active suitors – led to duels, lawsuits, and a brief imprisonment for our poet in 1634. Despite his gambling and amorous activities, he still found time to write, and had a play, *Aglaura*, performed by the King's Company in 1638. This was then performed at Court in a revised version that converted the tragedy into a tragicomedy. In 1637 he also wrote a religious tract, *An Account of Religion by Reason*.

In 1638 Suckling was made a Gentleman of the Privy Chamber, indicating that his stock was high with the royal family. The initial unsuccessful foray with his own troops occurred in Scotland in 1639, but he was then commissioned as captain of a troop of carabineers in 1640. He was soon also elected to Parliament but held his seat only briefly in the "Short Parliament" (1640). His politicking was soon to see him involved in the plot to free the King's adviser, the Earl of Strafford (Sir Thomas Wentworth) from the Tower, to which Strafford had been condemned for treason after falling out with Parliament. It was a sign of the times that, despite the King's support of Strafford, he was forced by Parliament to sign the Earl's death-warrant. Suckling's involvement in the rescue plot was evidently serious, as a warrant for his arrest was issued (along with others, including one for his friend and fellow-poet, William Davenant). Suckling was subsequently convicted of high treason by the House of Commons in August 1641. By this time he had already fled to France, where he died not long after his arrival, possibly a suicide by poison (according to John Aubrey in his *Lives*), although other lurid accounts were given some credence at the time. Strafford was executed in May 1641, around the time of Suckling's flight. When King Charles I followed him to the gallows nine years later, among his last words were that God had permitted his execution as punishment for his having consented to Strafford's death: "that unjust sentence which I suffered to take effect".

Suckling's poetry, as was common at this time, was collected by his friends and admirers after his death and published in three volumes; *Fragmenta Aurea* (1646), *The Last Remains of Sir John Suckling* (1659) and *The Works of Sir John Suckling* (1676, reissued 1696). Some of the works collected in these volumes are not now accepted by scholars as Suckling's, confusion no doubt arising from poems by others having been copied out in Suckling's hand, or by similarities of style.

There is a good modern edition (1971) of Suckling's works – now out of print, alas – from Oxford University Press, and the text here follows that edition in cases of doubt. Facsimiles of the first editions of *Fragmenta Aurea* and *The Last Remains* were also consulted during the preparation of this volume. Poems left out of this edition are those that are commonly accepted as not being by Suckling, despite their appearance in the posthumous collections. The text here is unmodernised – our standard practice where a good edition is no longer in print. The only exceptions to this rule have been to abandon the "long S" in favour of its modern iteration, the replacement of VV with modern W, and to expand period abbreviations, such as wth for *with*.

Tony Frazer

His Dream

On a still, silent night, scarce could I number
One of the clock, but that a golden slumber
Had locked my senses fast, and carried me
Into a world of blest felicitie,
I know not how: First to a Garden, where
The Apricock, the Cherry, and the Peare,
The Strawberry, and Plumb, were fairer far
Than that eye-pleasing Fruit that caus'd the jar
Betwixt the Goddesses, and tempted more
Than fair *Atlanta's* Ball, though gilded ore.
I gaz'd a while on these, and presently
A Silver-stream ran softly gliding by,
Upon whose banks, Lillies more white than snow
New faln from heaven, with Violets mixt, did grow;
Whose scent so chaf'd the neighbor air, that you
Would surely swear that Arabick spices grew
Not far from thence, or that the place had been
With Musk prepar'd, to entertain Loves Queen.
Whilst I admir'd, the River past away,
And up a Grove did spring, green as in *May*,
When *April* had been moist; upon whose bushes
The pretty Robins, Nightingals, and Thrushes,
Warbled their Notes so sweetly, that my ears
Did judge at least the musick of the Sphears.
But here my gentle Dream conveyed me
Into the place where I most long'd to see,
My Mistress bed; who, some few blushes past,
And smiling frowns, contented was at last
To let me touch her neck; I not content
With that, slippt to her breast, thence lower went,
And then——I awak'd.

A Supplement of an imperfect Copy of Verses of Mr. Will. Shakespears, By the Author

1.

One of her hands, one of her cheeks lay under,
    Cozening the pillow of a lawful kisse,
Which therefore swel'd, and seem'd to part asunder,
    As angry to be rob'd of such a blisse:
        The one lookt pale, and for revenge did long,
        While t'other blusht, 'cause it had done the wrong.

2.

Out of the bed the other fair hand was
    On a green sattin quilt, whose perfect white
Lookt like a Dazie in a field of grasse,*
    And shew'd like unmelt snow unto the sight:
        There lay this pretty perdue, safe to keep
        The rest oth' body that lay fast asleep.

3.

Her eyes (and therefore it was night) close laid,
    Strove to imprison beauty till the morn;
But yet the doors were of such fine stuffe made,
    That it broke through, and shew'd itself in scorn,
        Throwing a kind of light about the place,
        Which turn'd to smiles still as't came near her face.

4.

Her beams (which some dull men call'd hair) divided:
    Part with her cheeks, part with her lips did sport,
But these, as rude, her breath put by; some guided
    Wiselyer downwards sought, but falling short,
        Curl'd back in rings, and seem'd to turn agen
        To bite the part so unkindly held them in.

Shakespeare up to this point.

Love's Representation

Leaning her head upon my Brest,
There on Loves Bed she lay to rest;
My panting heart rock'd her asleep,
My heedful eyes the watch did keep:
Then Love by me being harbored there,
(No hope to be his Harbinger)
Desire his rival, kept the door;
For this of him I begg'd no more,
But that, our Mistress to entertain,
Some pretty fancy he would frame,
And represent it in a dream.
Of which my self should give the Theam.
Then first these thoughts I bid him show,
Which onely he and I did know,
Arrayed in duty and respect,
And not in Fancies that reflect:
Then those of value next present,
Approv'd by all the World's consent;
But to distinguish mine asunder,
Apparell'd they must be in wonder.
Such a device then I would have,
As Service not reward should crave,
Attir'd in spotless Innocence,
Not self-respect, nor no pretence:
Then such a Faith I would have shown,
As heretofore was never known.
Cloth'd with a constant clear intent,
Professing always as it meant.
And if Love no such Garments have,
My mind a Wardrobe is so brave,
That there sufficient he may see
To cloath Impossibility.
Then beamy Fetters he shall finde,
By admiration subt'ly twin'd,
That will keep fast the wanton'st thought,

That ere Imagination wrought:
There he shall find of Joy a chain,
Fram'd by despair of her disdain,
So curiously that it can tie
The smallest hopes that Thoughts now spie.
There acts as glorious as the Sun,
Are by her veneration spun,
In one of which I would have brought
A pure unspotted abstract thought
Considering her as she is good,
Not in her frame of Flesh and Blood.
These Attoms then, all in her sight
I bad him join, that so she might
Discern between true Loves Creation,
And that Loves form that's now in fashion.
Love granting unto my request
Began to labor in my Brest;
But with this motion he did make,
It heav'd so high that she did wake,
Blush'd at the favor she had done,
Then smil'd, and then away did run.

[A Barley-break]

1.
Love, Reason, Hate, did once bespeak
Three mates to play at barley-break;
Love, Folly took; and Reason, Fancy;
And Hate consorts with Pride; so dance they:
Love coupled last, and so it fell,
That Love and Folly were in hell.

2.
They break, and Love would Reason meet,
But Hate was nimbler on her feet;
Fancy looks for Pride, and thither
Hyes, and they two hugge together:
Yet this new coupling still doth tell
That Love and Folly were in hell.

3.
The rest do break again, and Pride
Hath now got Reason on her side;
Hate and Fancy meet, and stand
Untoucht by Love in Folly's hand:
Folly was dull, but Love ran well,
So Love and Folly were in hell.

A Candle

There is a thing which in the Light
Is seldom us'd, but in the Night
It serves the Maiden Female crew,
The Ladies, and the Good-wives too:
They use to take it in their hand,
And then it will uprightly stand;
And to a hole they it apply,
Where by its good will it would dye;
It spends, goes out, and still within
It leaves its moisture thick and thin.

A Pedler of Small-Wares

1.

A PEDLER I am, that take great care
And mickle pains for to sell Small-ware:
I had need do so, when women do buy,
That in small wares trade so unwillingly.

2.
L.W.

A Looking-glass, wilt please you Madam, buy?
A rare one 'tis indeed, for in it I
Can show what all the world besides can't do,
A Face like to your own, so fair, so true.

3.
L.E.

For you a Girdle, Madam? but I doubt me
Nature hath order'd there's no Waste about ye;
Pray therefore be but pleas'd to search my Pack,
There's no ware that I have that you shall lack.

4.
L.E. L.M.

You Ladies, want you Pins? if that you do,
I have those will enter, and that stifly too:
It's time you choose, in troth; you will bemone
Too late your tarrying, when my Pack's once gone.

5.
L.B. L.A.

As for you, Ladies, there are those behind
Whose ware perchance may better take your mind;
One cannot please ye all; the Pedler will draw back,
And wish against himself, that they may have the knack.

A Soldier

I am a man of war and might,
  And know thus much, that I can fight,
Whether I am i'th' wrong or right,
                            devoutly.

No woman under heaven I fear,
New Oaths I can exactly swear,
And forty Healths my brain will bear
                            most stoutly.

I cannot speak, but I can doe
As much as any of our crew;
And if you doubt it, some of you
                            may prove me.

I dare be bold thus much to say,
If that my bullets do but play,
You would be hurt so night and day,
                            Yet love me.

A Barber

I am a barber, and I'de have you know,
A Shaver too, sometimes no mad one though:
The reason why you see me now thus bare,
Is 'cause I always trade against the haire.
But yet I keep a state; who comes to me,
Whose're he is, he must uncover'd be.
When I'm at work, I'm bound to find discourse
To no great purpose, of great *Sweden* force.
Of *Witel*, and the Burse, and what 'twill cost
To get that back which was this Summer lost.
So fall to praising of his Lordships haire,
Ne'r so deform'd, I swear 'tis *sans* compare:
I tell him that the Kings doth sit no fuller,
And yet his is not half so good a color:
Then reach a pleasing Glass, that's made to lye
Like to its Master, most notoriously:
And if he must his Mistress see that day,
I with a Powder send him strait away.

Perjury [disdain'd]

Alas it is too late! I can no more
Love now, than I have lov'd before:
My *Flora*, 'tis my fate, not I;
And what you call Contempt, is Destiny.
I am no Monster sure, I cannot show
Two hearts; one I already ow:
And I have bound my self with oaths, and vowed
Oftener I fear than Heaven hath ere allowed,
That Faces now should work no more on me,
Than if they could not charm, or I not see.
And shall I break them? shall I think you can
Love, if I could, so foul a perjur'd man?
O no, 'tis equally impossible that I
Should love again, or you love Perjury.

Loves World

1.

In each mans heart that doth begin
To Love, there's ever fram'd within
A little world, for so I found
When first my passion reason drown'd.

2.

Instead of *Earth* unto this frame,   *Earth*
I had a faith was still the same,
For to be right it doth behoove
It be as that, fixt and not move;

3.

Yet as the Earth may sometime shake
(For winds shut up will cause a quake)
So, often jealousie, and fear,
Stolne into mine, cause tremblings there.

4.

My *Flora* was my *Sun*, for as   *Sunne*
One *Sun*, so but one *Flora* was:
All other faces borrowed hence
Their light and grace, as stars do thence.

5.

My hopes I call my *Moon*; for they,   *Moon*
Inconstant still, were at no stay;
But, as my Sun inclin'd to me,
Or more or less were sure to be:

6.

Sometimes it would be full, and then
Oh! too too soon decrease agen;
Eclip'st sometimes, that 't would so fall
There would appear no hope at all.

7.

My thoughts, 'cause infinite they be
Must be those many *Stars* we see;   *Starres*
Of which some wandred at their will,
But most on her were *fixed* still.   *Fixed Planets*

8.

My burning flame and hot desire   *Element*
Must be the *Element of Fire*,   *of fire*
Which hath as yet so secret been
That it as that was never seen:

9.

No Kitching fire, nor eating flame,
But innocent, hot but in name;
A fire that's starv'd when fed, and gone
When too much fewel is laid on.

10.

But as it plainly doth appear,
That fire subsists by being near
The Moons bright Orbe, so I beleeve
Ours doth, for hope keeps love alive.

11.

My fancy was the *Ayre*, most free   *Ayre*
And full of mutability,
Big with Chimera's, vapours here
Innumerable hatcht as there.

12.

The *Sea's* my mind, which calm would be   *Sea*
Were it from winds (my passions) free;
But out alas! no *Sea* I find
Is troubled like a Lovers mind.

13.
Within it Rocks and Shallows be,
Despair and fond credulity.

14.
But in this world it were good reason
We did distinguish Time and Season;
Her presence then did make the *Day*,
And *Night* shall come when shee's away.

15.
Long absence in far distant place
Creates the *Winter*, and the space   *Winter*
She tarryed with me; well I might
Call it my *Summer* of delight.   *Summer*

16.
Diversity of weather came
From what she did, and thence had name;
Sometimes sh'would smile, that made it fair;
And when she laught, the Sun shin'd clear.

17.
Sometimes sh'would frown, and sometimes weep,
So Clouds and Rain their turns do keep;
Sometimes again sh'would be all ice,
Extreamly cold, extreamly nice.

18.
But soft my Muse, the world is wide,
And all at once was not descride:
It may fall out some honest Lover
The rest hereafter will discover.

The Metamorphosis

The little Boy, to shew his might and power,
Turn'd Io to a Cow, *Narcissus* to a flower;
Transformed *Apollo* to a homely Swain,
And *Jove* himself into a Golden Rain.
    These shapes were tolerable, but by th' Mass
    He's metamorphos'd me into an Ass!

To B. C.

When first, fair Mistress, I did see your face,
I brought, but carried no eyes from the place:
And since that time God *Cupid* hath me led,
In hope that once I shall enjoy your bed.
    But I despair; for now alas I find,
    Too late for me, The blind does lead the blind.

Lutea Allison:
Si sola es, nulla es

Though you *Diana*-like have liv'd still chast,
   Yet must you not (Fair) die a Maid at last:
The roses on your cheeks were never made
To bless the eye alone, and so to fade;
Nor had the cherries on your lips their being
To please no other sense than that of seeing:
You were not made to look on, though that be
A bliss too great for poor mortalitie:
In that alone those rarer parts you have,
To better uses sure wise Nature gave
Than that you put them to; to love, to wed,
For *Hymens* rites, and for the Marriage-bed
You were ordain'd, and not to lie alone;
One is no number, till that two be one.
To keep a maidenhead but till fifteen.
Is worse than murder, and a greater sin
Than to have lost it in the lawful sheets
With one that should want skill to reap those sweets:
But not to lose't at all, by *Venus*, this,
And by her son, inexpiable is;
And should each Female guilty be o'th' crime,
The world would have its end before its time.

Upon the first sight of my Lady Seimor

Wonder not much, if thus amaz'd I look,
    Since I saw you, I have been Planet-strook:
A Beauty, and so rare I did descrie,
As, should I set her forth, you all as I,
Would lose your hearts; for he that can
Know her and live, he must be more than man.
An apparition of so sweet a Creature,
That credit me, she had not any feature
That did not speak her Angel. But no more
Such heavenly things as these we must adore,
Nor prattle of; lest when we do but touch.
Or strive to know, we wrong her too too much.

Non est mortale quod opto:
Upon Mrs A. L.

Thou thinkst I flatter when thy praise I tell,
    But thou dost all Hyperboles excell:
For I am sure thou art no Mortal creature,
But a Divine one thron'd in human feature.
Thy piety is such, that heaven by merit,
If ever any did, thou shouldst inherit:
Thy modesty is such, that hadst thou bin
Tempted as *Eve*, thou wouldst have shunn'd her sin:
So lovely fair thou art, that sure Dame Nature
Meant thee the pattern of the Female creature:
Besides all this, thy flowing wit is such,
That were it not in thee, 't had bin too much
For Woman-kind: should Envy look thee ore,
It would confess thus much, if not much more.
I love thee well, yet wish some bad in thee,
For sure I am thou art too good for me.

Upon A. M.

Yeeld not, my Love; but be as coy,
As if thou knew'st not how to toy:
The Fort resign'd with ease, men Cowards prove
And lazie grow. Let me besiege thy Love,
Let me despair at least three times a day,
And take repulses upon each essay:
If I but ask a kiss, straight blush as red
As if I tempted for thy maidenhead:
Contract thy smiles, if that they go too far,
And frown as much as if you meant to mar
That Face, which Nature sure intended
Should ne'r be marr'd, because't could ne'r be mended.
Take no corruption from thy Grandame *Eve*;
Rather want faith to save thee, then believe
Too soon: For credit me 'tis true,
Men most enjoy, when least they doe.

Upon Sir John Laurence's bringing Water over the hills to my Lord Middlesex his House at Wiston

And is the water come? sure't cannot be,
It runs too much against Philosophie;
For heavy bodies to the Centre bend,
Light bodies only naturally ascend.
How comes this then to pass? The good Knights skill
Could nothing do without the Waters will:
    Then 'twas the Waters love that made it flow,
    For Love will creep where well it cannot go.

A Prologue of the Author's to a Masque at Wiston

Expect not here a curious River fine,
Our wits are short of that: alas the time!
The neat refined language of the Court
We know not; if we did, our Country sport
Must not be too ambitious; 'tis for kings,
Not for their Subjects, to have such rare things.
Besides though, I confess, *Parnassus* hardly,
Yet *Helicon* this Summer-time is dry:
Our wits were at an ebbe or very low,
And, to say troth, I think they cannot flow.
But yet a gracious influence from you
May alter Nature in our Brow-sick crew.
Have patience then, we pray, and sit a while;
And, if a laugh be too much, lend a smile.

To my Lady E. C. at her going out of England

I must confess, when I did part from you,
I could not force an artificial dew
Upon my cheeks, nor with a gilded phrase
Express how many hundred several ways
My heart was tortur'd, nor with arms across
In discontented garbs set forth my loss:
Such loud expressions many times do come
From lightest hearts: great griefs are always dumb;
The shallow Rivers rore, the deep are still.
Numbers of painted words may shew much skill,
But little anguish; and a cloudy face
Is oft put on, to serve both time and place:
The blazing wood may to the eye seem great,
But 'tis the fire rak'd up that has the heat,
And keeps it long. True sorrow's like to wine,
That which is good does never need a signe.
My eyes were channels far too small to be
Conveyers of such floods of miserie:
And so pray think; or if you'd entertain
A thought more charitable, suppose some strain
Of sad repentance had, not long before,
Quite emptied for my sins that watry store.
So shall you him oblige that still will be
Your servant to his best abilitie.

A Song to a Lute

Hast thou seen the Doun ith' air,
    when wanton blasts have tost it;
Or the Ship on the Sea,
    when ruder winds have crost it?
Hast thou markt the Crocodiles weeping,
    or the Foxes sleeping?
Or hast view'd the Peacock in his pride,
    or the Dove by his Bride.
    when he courts for his leachery?
Oh, so fickle, oh so vain, oh so false, so false is she!

Upon my Lady Carliles walking in Hampton-Court garden

Dialogue
T[homas] C[arew].   J[ohn] S[uckling].

Thom.
Didst thou not find the place inspir'd,
And flow'rs, as if they had desir'd
No other Sun, start from their beds,
And for a sight steal out their heads?
Heardst thou not musick when she talk't?
And didst not find that as she walkt
She threw rare perfumes all about
Such as bean-blossoms newly out,
Or chafed spices give?——

J. S.
I must confesse those perfumes (*Tom*)
I did not smell; nor found that from
Her passing by, ought sprang up new:
The flow'rs had all their birth from you;
For I pass't o're the self same walk,
And did not find one single stalk
Of any thing that was to bring
This unknown after after-spring.

Thom.
Dull and insensible, could'st see
A thing so near a Deity
Move up and down, and feel no change?

J. S.
None, and so great, were alike strange;
I had my Thoughts, but not your way,
All are not born (Sir) to the Bay;
Alas! *Tom*, I am flesh and blood,

And was consulting how I could
In spite of masks and hoods descry
The parts deni'd unto the eye;
I was undoing all she wore,
And had she walkt but one turn more,
Eve in her first state had not been
More naked, or more plainly seen.

Thom.
'T was well for thee she left the place,
There is great danger in that face;
But had'st thou view'd her legg and thigh,
And upon that discovery
Search't after parts that are more dear,
(As Fancy seldom stops so near)
No time or age had ever seen
So lost a thing as thou hadst been.

J. S.
'Troth in her face I could descry
No danger, no divinity.
But since the pillars were so good
On which the lovely fountain stood,
Being once come so near, I think
I should have ventur'd hard to drink.
What ever fool like me had been
If I'd not done as well as seen?
There to be lost why should I doubt,
Where fools with ease go in and out?

Upon T. C. having the P.

Troth, *Tom*, I must confess I much admire
  Thy water should find passage through the fire:
For fire and water never could agree;
These now by nature have some sympathie:
Sure then his way he forces; for all know
The *French* ne'er grants a passage to his foe.
If it be so, his valor I must praise,
That being the weaker, yet can force his ways;
And wish that to his valor he had strength,
That he might drive the fire quite out at length:
For (troth) as yet the fire gets the day,
For evermore the water runs away.

Love's Burning-glass

Wondering long, how I could harmless see
  Men gazing on those beams that fired me,
At last I found, it was the Chrystal-love
Before my heart, that did the heat improve:
Which, by contracting of those scatter'd rayes
Into it self, did so produce my blaze.
Now lighted by my Love, I see the same
Beams dazzle those, that me are wont t'inflame,
And now I bless my Love, when I do think
By how much I had rather burn than wink.
But how much happier were it thus to burn,
If I had liberty to choose my urn!
But since those beams do promise only fire,
This flame shall purge me of the dross, Desire.

The Miracle

If thou bee'st Ice, I do admire
How thou couldst set my heart on fire;
Or how thy fire could kindle me,
Thou being Ice, and not melt thee;
But even my flames, light as thy own.
Have hardned thee into a stone!
Wonder of Love, that canst fulfil,
Inverting nature thus, thy will;
Making ice another burn,
Whilst it self doth harder turn!

The deformed Mistress

I know there are some Fools that care
Not for the body, so the face be faire:
Some others too that in a female creature
Respect not beauty, but a comely feature:
And others too, that for those parts in sight
Care not so much, so that the rest be right.
Each man his humor hath; and faith 'tis mine
To love that woman which I now define.
First I would have her Wainscot Face and Hand
More wrincled far than any pleited band,
That in those furrows, if I'de take the pains,
I might both sow and reap all sorts of grains:
Her Nose I'de have a foot long, not above,
With pimples embroder'd, for those I love;
And at the end a comely Pearl of Snot,
Considering whether it should fall or not:
Provided next that half her Teeth be out,
I do not care much if her pretty Snout
Meet with her furrow'd chin, and both together
Hem in her Lips, as dry as good whit-leather:
One Wall-Eye she shall have; for that's a signe
In other Beasts the best, why not in mine?
Her Neck I'le have to be pure Jet at least,
With yellow spots enamell'd; and her Breast
Like a Grashoppers wing, both thin and lean,
Not to be toucht for dirt, unless swept clean:
As for her Belly, 'tis no matter so
There be a Belly, and a Cunt below;
Yet if you will, let it be something high,
And always let there be a timpanie.
But soft, where am I now? here I should stride,
Lest I fall in, the place must be so wide;
And pass unto her Thighs, which shall be just
Like to an Ants that's scraping in the dust:
Into her Legs I'de have Loves issue fall,

And all her Calf into a gouty Small:
Her Feet both thick and Eagle like displaid,
The symptoms of a comely handsom maid.
As for her parts behind, I ask no more,
If they but answer those that are before,
I have my utmost wish; and having so.
Judge whether I am happy, yea or no.

Upon L[ady] M[iddlesex] Weeping

Whoever was the cause your tears were shed,
   May these my curses light upon his head:
May he be first in love, and let it be
With a most known and black Deformitie,
Nay far surpass all Witches that have been,
Since our first parents taught us how to sin!
Then let this Hag be coy, and he run mad
For that which no man else would ere have had:
And in this fit may he commit the thing
May him impenitent to th' gallows bring!
Then might he for one tear his pardon have,
But want that single grief his life to save!
And being dead, may he at heaven venter,
But for the guilt of this one fact ne'r enter.

Detraction Execrated

1.

Thou vermin Slander, bred in abject minds
  Of thoughts impure, by vile tongues animate,
Canker of conversation! couldst thou find
Nought but our Love, whereon to show thy hate?
Thou never wert, when we two were alone;
What canst thou witness then? thy base dull aid
Was useless in our conversation,
Where each meant more, then could by both be said.

2.

Whence hadst thou thy intelligence, from earth?
That part of us ne'r knew that we did love:
Or from the air? Our gentle sighs had birth
From such sweet raptures as to joy did move:
Our thoughts, as pure as the chaste Mornings breath,
When from the Nights cold arms it creeps away,
Were cloth'd in words, and Maidens blush that hath
More purity, more innocence than they.

3.

Nor from the water couldst thou have this tale;
No briny tear hath furrow'd her smooth cheek;
And I was pleas'd; I pray what should he aile
That had her Love, for what else could he seek?
We shortned days to moments by Loves art,
Whilst our two souls in amorous extasie
Perceiv'd no passing time, as if a part
Our love had been of still Eternity.

4.

Much less could have it from the purer fire:
Our heat exhales no vapor from coarse sense,
Such as are hopes, or fears, or fond desires;
Our mutual Love it self did recompence.

Thou hast no correspondence in heaven,
And th'elemental world thou seest is free:
Whence hadst thou then this talking, Monster? even
From hell, a harbor fit for it and thee.

5.

Curst be th'officious Tongue that did address
Thee to her ears, to ruine my content:
May it one minute taste such happiness,
Deserving lose't, unpittied it lament!
I must forbear her sight, and so repay
In grief those hours Joy shortened to a dram:
Each minute I will lengthen to a day,
And in one year outlive *Methusalem*.

On King Richard the third, who lies buried under Leicester bridge

What meanes this watry Canop' bout thy bed,
These streaming vapours o're thy sinfull head,
Are they thy teares? alasse in vaine they're spilt,
'Tis now too late to wash away thy guilt:
Thou still art bloudy *Richard*, and 'tis much,
The water should not from thy very touch,
Turne quite Egyptian, and the scaly frye
Feare to be kild, and so they carkise flye.
Bathe, bathe they fill, and take thy pleasure now
In this cold bed, yet guilty *Richard* know
Judgement must come, and water then will be
A Heaven to thee in hellish miserye.

Against Fruition [I]

1.
Stay here, fond youth, and ask no more, be wise,
Knowing too much long since lost Paradise;
The vertuous joyes thou hast, thou would'st should still
Last in their pride; and would'st not take it ill
If rudely from sweet dreams (and for a toy)
Th'wert wak't? he wakes himself, that does enjoy.

2.
Fruition adds no new wealth, but destroyes,
And while it pleaseth much the palate, cloyes;
Who thinks he shall be happyer for that,
As reasonably might hope he should grow fat
By eating to a Surfet: this once past,
What relishes? even kisses lose their tast.

3.
Urge not 'tis necessary, alas! we know
The homeliest thing which mankind does is so;
The World is of a vast extent we see,
And must be peopled; Children then must be;
So must bread too; but since there are enough
Born to the drudgery, what need we plough?

4.
Women enjoy'd (what s'ere before th'ave been)
Are like Romances read, or sights once seen:
Fruition's dull, and spoils the Play much more
Than if one read or knew the plot before;
'Tis expectation makes a blessing dear:
It were not heaven, if we knew what it were.

5.
And as in Prospects we are there pleas'd most
Where somthing keeps the eye from being lost,

And leaves us room to guesse, so here restraint
Holds up delight, that with excesse would faint.
They who know all the wealth they have, are poor,
He's onely rich that cannot tell his store.

Against Fruition [II]

Fye upon hearts that burn with mutual fire;
I hate two minds that breathe but one desire;
Were I to curse th'unhallow'd sort of men,
I'de wish them to love, and be lov'd agen.
Love's a *Camelion*, that lives on meer ayre,
And surfets when it comes to grosser fare:
'Tis petty Jealousies, and little fears,
Hopes joyn'd with doubts, and joyes with *April* tears,
That crowns our Love with pleasures: these are gone
When once we come to full *Fruition*;
Like waking in a morning, when all night
Our fancy hath been fed with true delight.
O! what a stroke 'twould be! Sure I should die,
Should I but hear my mistresse once say, I.
That monster Expectation feeds too high
For any woman e're to satisfie:
And no brave Spirit ever car'd for that.
Which in Down-beds with ease he could come at.
Shee's but an honest whore that yeelds, although
She be as cold as ice, as pure as snow:
He that enjoys her hath no more to say
But keep us Fasting, if you'll have us pray.
Then fairest Mistresse, hold the power you have,
By still denying what we still do crave:
In keeping us in hopes strange things to see
That never were, nor are, nor e're shall be.

To Mr Davenant for Absence

Wonder not, if I stay not here,
   Hurt lovers (like to wounded Deer)
Must shift the place; for standing still
Leaves too much time to know our ill:
Where there is a Traytor eye,
That lets in from th'enemy
All that may supplant an heart,
'Tis time the Chief should use some Art:
Who parts the object from the sence,
Wisely cuts off intelligence.
O how quickly men must die,
Should they stand all Loves Battery!
Persinda's eyes great mischief do,
So does (we know) the Canon too;
But men are safe at distance still:
Where they reach not, they cannot kill.
Love is a fit, and soon is past,
Ill dyet onely makes it last;
Who is still looking, gazing ever,
Drinks wine i'th' very height o'th' Fever.

Against Absence

My whining Lover, what needs all
These vows of life Monastical?
Despairs, retirements, jealousies,
And subtile sealing up of eyes?
Come, come, be wise, return again;
A finger burnt's as great a pain;
And the same Physick, self same art
Cures that, would cure a flaming heart,
Would'st thou, whilst yet the fire is in
But hold it to the fire again.
If you (Dear Sir) the plague have got,
What matter is't whether or not
They let you in the same house lie,
Or carry you abroad to die?
He whom the plague or Love once takes,
Every Room a Pest-House makes.
Absence were good if't were but sence,
That onely held th'Intelligence:
Pure love alone no hurt would do;
But love is love, and magick too;
Brings a mistresse thousand miles,
And the sleight of locks beguiles,
Makes her entertain thee there,
And the same time your Rival here;
And (oh! the divel) that she should
Say finer things now then she would;
So nobly Fancy doth supply
What the dull sence lets fall and die.
Beauty, like mans old enemy's known
To tempt him most when he's alone:
The ayre of some wild o'regrown wood
Or pathlesse Grove is the Boyes food.
Return then back, and feed thine eye,
Feed all thy sences, and feast high.
Spare dyet is the cause Love lasts,
For Surfets sooner kill than Fasts.

[To his Rival 1]

My dearest Rival, least our Love
Should with excentrique motion move,
Before it learn to go astray,
Wee'l teach and set it in a way,
And such directions give unto't,
That it shall never wander foot.
Know first then, we will serve as true
For one poor smile, as we would do,
If we had what our higher flame,
Or our vainer wish could frame.
Impossible shall be our hope;
And Love shall onely have his scope
To joyn with Fancy now and then,
And think what Reason would condemn:
And on these grounds wee'l love as true,
As if they were most sure t'ensue;
And chastly for these things wee'l stay,
As if to morrow were the day.
Mean time we two will teach our hearts
In Lovers burdens bear their parts:
Thou first shall sigh, and say shee's fair,
And I'le still answer, past compare;
Thou shalt set out each part o'th' face,
While I extol each little grace;
Thou shalt be ravisht at her wit,
And I, that she so governs it;
Thou shalt like well that hand, that eye,
That lip, that look, that majesty;
And in good language them adore:
While I want words, and do it more.
Yea we will sit and sigh a while,
And with soft thoughts some time beguil;
But straight again break out, and praise
All we had done before, new-waies.
Thus will we do till paler death

Come with a warrant for our breath;
And then whose fate shall be to die
First of us two, by Legacy
Shall all his store bequeath, and give
His love to him that shall survive;
For no one stock can ever serve
To love so much as shee'l deserve.

To his Rival [II]

Now we have taught our Love to know
   That it must creep where't cannot go,
And be for once content to live,
Since here it cannot have to thrive;
It will not be amisse t'enquire
What fuel should maintain this fire:
For fires do either flame too high,
Or where they cannot flame they die.
First then (my half but better heart)
Know this must wholly be her part:
(For thou and I, like Clocks, are wound
Up to the height, and must move round;)
She then by still denying what
We fondly crave, shall such a rate
Set on each trifle, that a kisse
Shall come to be the utmost blisse.
Where sparks and fire do meet with tinder,
Those sparks meer fire will still engender:
To make this good, no debt shall be
From service or fidelity;
For she shall ever pay that score,
By onely bidding us do more:
So (though she still a niggard be)
In graceing, where none's due, shee's free.
The favors she shall cast on us,

(Least we should grow presumptuous)
Shall not with too much love be shown,
Nor yet the common way still done;
But ev'ry smile and little glance
Shall look half lent, and half by chance:
The Ribbon, Fan, or Muffe that she
Would should be kept by thee or me,
Should not be giv'n before too many,
But neither thrown to's, when there's any;
So that herself should doubtful be
Whether 'twere fortune flung't, or she.
She shall not like the thing we do
Sometimes, and yet shall like it too;
Nor any notice take at all
Of what, we gone, she would extol:
Love she shall feed, but fear to nourish,
For where fear is, love cannot flourish;
Yet live it must, nay must and shall,
While *Desdemona* is at all:
But when she's gone, then Love shall die,
And in her grave buried lie.

To a Lady that forbidd to love before Company

What noe more favours, not A Ribbon more,
Not fanne, nor muffe to hold as heretofore?
Must all those little blisses then be left,
And evert kisse wee have become a theft?
May we not looke our selves into a Traunce,
Let our soules parly at our eyes, not glaunce,
Not touch the hand, nor by soft wringing there
Whisper a love that none but eyes can heare?
Not free a sighe, A sighe that's there for you,
Deare must I love you, yet not love you too?
Bee not so nice Faire, sooner shall they Trace
The featherd Travellers from place to place,
By prints they leave i'th' Ayre, and sooner say
By what right line the last starre made his way
That fledd from heaven to us, then guesse or know
How our loves first did spring, or how they grow;
Love is all spirit, fayries sooner may
Bee taken Tardy, when they night-tricks play,
Than wee; we are too safe I feare, that rather,
Would they could finde us both in bedd together!

The Invocation

1.

Ye juster Powers of Love and Fate,
Give me the reason why
    A Lover crost
    And all hopes lost
May not have leave to dye.

2.

It is but just, and Love needs must
Confess it is his part,
    When he doth spie
    One wounded lie,
To pierce the others heart.

3.

But yet if he so cruel be
To have one breast to hate,
    If I must live
    And thus survive,
How far more cruel's Fate?

4.

In this same state I find too late
I am; and here's the grief:
    Cupid can cure,
    Death heal I'm sure,
Yet neither sends relief.

5.

To love, or die, beg onely I:
Just Powers, some end me give;
    And Traitor-like
    Thus force me not
Without a heart to live.

The Expostulation [I]

1.
Tell me ye juster Deities,
That pitty Lovers miseries,
Why should my own unworthiness
Fright me to seek my happiness?
It is as natural as just,
Him for to love, whom needs I must:
All men confess that love's a fire,
Then who denies it to aspire?

2.
Tell me, if thou wert Fortunes thrall,
Wouldst thou not raise thee from the fall?
Seek only to orelook thy state
Whereto thou art condemn'd by Fate?
Then let me love my *Coridon*,
And by Love's leave, him love alone:
For I have read of Stories oft,
That Love hath wings and soars aloft.

3.
Then let me grow in my desire,
Though I be martyr'd in that fire:
For grace it is enough for me
But only to love such as he:
For never shall my thoughts be base,
Though luckless, yet without disgrace:
Then let him that my Love shall blame,
Or clip Loves wings, or quench Loves flame.

[The Expostulation II]

1.

Unjust Decrees! that do at once exact,
From such a Love as worthy hearts should own,
  So wild a passion,
  And yet so tame a presence
   As holding no proportion
Changes into impossible obedience:

2.

Let it suffice, that neither I do love
In such a calm observance, as to weigh
  Each word I say,
  And each examin'd look t'approve
   That towards her doth move,
  Without so much of fire
As might in time kindle into desire;

3.

Or give me leave to burst into a flame,
And at the scope of my unbounded will
  Love her my fill;
  No superscriptions of Fame,
   Of honor, or good name,
  No thought but to improve
The gentle and quick approaches of my Love.

4.

But thus to throng and overlade a soul
With Love, and then to leave a room for fear,
  That shall all that controll,
  What is it but to rear
   Our passions and our hopes on high,
  That thence they may descrie
The noblest way how to despair and die?

Sonnet I

1.

Do'st see how unregarded now
    that piece of beauty passes?
There was a time when I did vow
    to that alone;
    But mark the fate of faces:
The red and white works now no more on me
Then if it could not charm or I not see.

2.

And yet the face continues good,
    and I have still desires,
Am still the self same flesh and blood,
    as apt to melt
    and suffer from those fires;
Oh! some kind power unriddle where it lies,
Whether my heart be faulty, or her eyes?

3.

She every day her Man does kill,
    and I as often die;
Neither her power, then, nor my will
    can question'd be,
    what is the mystery?
Sure Beauties Empires, like to greater States
Have certain periods set, and hidden fates.

Sonnet II

1.

Of thee (kind boy) I ask no red and white
    to make up my delight,
    no odd becomming graces,
Black eyes, or little know-not-whats, in faces;
Make me but mad enough, give me good store
Of Love, for her I Court,
              I ask no more,
'Tis love in love that makes the sport.

2.

There's no such thing as that we beauty call,
    it is meer cousenage all;
    for though some long ago
Like't certain colours mingled so and so,
That doth not tie me now from chusing new;
If I a fancy take
              To black and blue,
That fancy doth it beauty make.

3.

'Tis not the meat, but 'tis the appetite
    makes eating a delight,
    and if I like one dish
More than another, that a Pheasant is;
What in our watches, that in us is found,
So to the height and nick
              We up be wound,
No matter by what hand or trick.

Sonnet III

1.

Oh! for some honest Lovers ghost,
    Some kind unbodied post
  Sent from the shades below.
  I strangely long to know
Whether the nobler Chaplets wear,
Those that their mistresse scorn did bear,
    Or those that were us'd kindly.

2.

For what-so-e're they tell us here
    To make those sufferings dear,
  'Twill there I fear be found,
  That to the being crown'd
T'have loved alone will not suffice,
Unlesse we also have been wise,
    And have our Loves enjoy'd.

3.

What posture can we think him in,
    That here unlov'd agen
  Departs, and's thither gone,
  Where each sits by his own?
Or how can that *Elizium* be,
Where I my Mistresse still must see
    Circled in others Armes?

4.

For there the Judges all are just,
    And *Sophonisba* must
  Be his whom she held dear;
  Not his who lov'd her here:
The sweet *Philoclea*, since she dy'de
Lies by her *Pirocles* his side,
    Not by *Amphialus*.

  Some Bayes (perchance) or Myrtle bough
    For difference crowns the brow
    Of those kind souls that were
    The noble Martyrs here;
And if that be the onely odds,
(As who can tell) ye kinder Gods,
    Give me the Woman here.

[Love's Sanctuary]

1.
The crafty Boy that had full oft assay'd
  To peirce my stubborn and resisting Brest,
(But still the bluntness of his Darts betrayed)
Resolv'd at last of setting up his rest
    Either my wilde unruly heart to tame,
    Or quit his Godhead, and his Bow disclaim.

2.
So all his lovely Looks, his pleasing Fires;
All his sweet Motions, all his taking Smiles;
All that awakes, all that inflames Desires;
All that by force Commands, all that beguiles:
    He does into one pair of Eyes convey,
    And there begs leave that he himself may stay.

3.
And there he brings me, where his ambush lay,
Secure and careless, to a stranger Land;
And never warning me, which was foul play,
Does make me close by all this Beauty stand,
    Where first struck dead, I did at last recover,
    To know that I might onely live to love her.

4.
So I'll be sworn I do, and do confess
The blinde Lads power, whilst he inhabits there;
But I'll be even with him neretheless,
If ere I chance to meet with him elsewhere.
    If other eyes invite the Boy to tarry,
    I'll flie to hers as to a Sanctuary.

[Loves Feast]

1.
I pray thee spare me, gentle Boy,
Presse me no more for that slight toy,
That foolish trifle of an heart;
I swear it will not do its part,
Though thou dost thine, employ'st thy power and art.

2.
For through long custom it has known
The little secrets, and is grown
Sullen and wise, will have its will,
And like old Hawks pursues that still
That makes least sport, flies onely where't can kill.

3.
Some youth that has not made his story,
Will think perchance the pain's the glory,
And mannerly sit out Loves Feast;
I shall be carving of the best,
Rudely call for the last course 'fore the rest.

4.
And oh! when once that course is past,
How short a time the Feast doth last!
Men rise away, and scarce say grace,
Or civilly once thank the face
That did invite, but seek another place.

[Loves Offence]

1.

If when Don *Cupids* dart
Doth wound a heart,
    we hide our grief
    and shun relief,
The smart increaseth on that score;
For wounds unsearcht but rankle more.

2.

Then if we whine, look pale,
And tell our tale,
    men are in pain
    for us again;
So, neither speaking doth become
The Lovers state, nor being dumb.

3.

When this I do descry,
Then thus think I,
    love is the fart
    of every heart:
It pains a man when 'tis kept close,
And others doth offend, when 'tis let loose.

[Desdain]

    A quoy servent tant d'artifices
Et des semens aux vents jettez
Si vos amours et vos services
Me sont des importunitez.

    L'amour à d'autres voeux m'appelle
N'attendez jamais rien de moy,
Ne pensez nous rendre infidelle,
En me tesmoignant vostre foy.

    L'amant qui mon amour possede
Est trop plein de perfection:
Car doublement il vous excede
De merite et d'affection.

    Je n'en puis estre refroidie
Ny rompre un cordage si dous,
Ny le rompre sans perfidie
Ny d'estre perfide pour vous.

    Vos attentes sont toutes vaines,
Le vous dire, est vous obliger,
Pour vous faire estre de vos peines
De vous et du temps mesnager.

[Disdain]
Englished thus by the Author:

To what end serve the promises
    And oaths lost in the air?
Since all your proffer'd services
    To me but tortures are?

Another now enjoys my Love,
    Set you your heart at rest:
Think not me from my faith to move,
    Because you faith protest.

The man that doth possess my heart,
    Has twice as much perfection,
And does excell you in desert,
    As much as in affection.

I cannot break so sweet a bond,
    Unless I prove untrue:
Nor can I ever be so fond,
    To prove untrue for you.

Your attempts are but in vain,
    (To tell you is a favor:)
For things that may be, rack your brain;
    Then lose not thus your labor.

Profer'd Love rejected

1.

It is not four years ago,
    I offered Forty crowns
To lie with her a night or so:
    She answered me in frowns.

2.

Not two years since, she meeting me
    Did whisper in my eare,
That she would at my service be
    If I contented were.

3.

I told her I was cold as snow,
    And had no great desire;
But should be well content to go
    To Twenty, but no higher.

4.

Some three moneths since or thereabout,
    She that so coy had bin,
Bethought herself and found me out,
    And was content to sin.

5.

I smil'd at that, and told her I
    Did think it something late,
And that I'de not repentance buy
    At above half the rate.

6.

This present morning early she
    Forsooth came to my bed,
And *gratis* there she offered me
    Her high-priz'd maidenhead.

7.

I told her that I thought it then
    Far dearer than I did,
When I at first the Forty crowns
    For one nights lodging bid.

[The constant Lover]

Sir J. S.

1.

Out upon it, I have lov'd
    Three whole days together;
And am like to love three more,
    If it hold fair weather.

2.

Time shall moult away his wings
    Ere he shall discover
In the whole wide world agen
    Such a constant Lover.

3.

But a pox upon't, no praise
    There is due at all to me:
Love with me had made no stay,
    Had it any been but she.

4.

Had it any been but she
    And that very very Face,
There had been at least ere this
    A dozen dozen in her place.

[The Answer]

Sir Toby Matthews

1.
Say, but did you love so long?
    In troth I needs must blame you:
Passion did your Judgment wrong,
    Or want of Reason shame you.

2.
Truth, Times fair and witty Daughter,
    Quickly did discover,
You were a Subject fit for laughter,
    And more Fool then lover.

3.
But you needs must merit praise
    For your constant Folly,
Since you doted three whole dayes:
    Were you not melancholy?

4.
She to whom you were so true,
    And that very very Face,
Puts each minute such as you
    A dozen dozen to disgrace

The careless Lover

1.
Never believe me if I love,
 Or know what 'tis or mean to prove;
And yet in faith I lye, I do,
And she's extremely handsom too:
    She's fair, she's wondrous fair,
    But I care not who know it,
    Ere I'le die for love, I'le fairly forgo it.

2.
This heat of hope, or cold of fear,
My foolish heart could never bear:
One sigh imprison'd ruines more
Then earthquakes have done heretofore:
    She's fair, &c.

3.
When I am hungry, I do eat.
And cut no fingers 'stead of meat;
Nor with much gazing on her face
Do ere rise hungry from the place:
    She's fair, &c.

4.
A gentle round fill'd to the brink
To this and t'other Friend I drink;
And when 'tis nam'd anothers health,
I never make it hers by stealth:
    She's fair, &c.

5.
Black-Friars to me, and old *Whitehall,*
Is even as much as is the fall
Of fountains on a pathless grove,
And nourishes as much my love:
    She's fair, &c.

6.

I visit, talk, do business, play,
And for a need laugh out a day:
Who does not thus in *Cupids* school,
He makes not Love, but plays the Fool:
    She's fair, &c.

Song

1.

Honest Lover whosoever,
If in all thy love there ever
Was one wav'ring thought, if thy flame
Were not still even, still the same:
    Know this,
    Thou lov'st amisse,
    And to love true,
Thou must begin again, and love anew.

2.

If when she appears i'th' room,
Thou dost not quake, and are struck dumb,
And in striving this to cover
Dost not speak thy words twice over,
    Know this,
    Thou lov'st amisse,
    And to love true,
Thou must begin again, and love anew.

3.

If fondly thou dost not mistake,
And all defects for graces take,
Perswad'st thyself that jests are broken,
When she hath little or nothing spoken,
    Know this,

    Thou lov'st amisse,
    And to love true,
Thou must begin again, and love anew.

        4.
If when thou appear'st to be within,
Thou lett'st not men ask and ask agen,
And when thou answer'st, if it be
To what was askt thee, properly,
      Know this,
    Thou lov'st amisse,
    And to love true,
Thou must begin again, and love anew.

        5.
If when thy stomack calls to eat,
Thou cutt'st not fingers 'steed of meat,
And with much gazing on her face
Dost not rise hungry from the place,
      Know this,
    Thou lov'st amisse,
    And to love true,
Thou must begin again, and love anew.

        6.
If by this thou dost discover
That thou art no perfect Lover,
And desiring to love true,
Thou dost begin to love anew:
      Know this,
    Thou lov'st amisse,
    And to love true,
Thou must begin again, and love anew.

Loving and Beloved

1.
There never yet was honest man
    That ever drove the trade of love;
It is impossible, nor can
    Integrity our ends promove:
For Kings and Lovers are alike in this
That their chief art in reigne dissembling is.

2.
Here we are lov'd, and there we love;
    Good nature now and passion strive
Which of the two should be above,
    And laws unto the other give.
So we false fire with art sometimes discover,
And the true fire with the same art do cover.

3.
What Rack can Fancy find so high?
    Here we must Court, and here ingage,
Though in the other place we die.
    Oh! 'tis torture all, and cozenage;
And which the harder is I cannot tell,
To hide true love, or make false love look well.

4.
Since it is thus, God of desire,
    Give me my honesty again,
    And take thy brands back, and thy fire;
I'me weary of the State I'me in:
Since (if the very best should now befal),
Loves Triumph, must be Honours Funeral

[Womans Constancy]

1.
There never yet was woman made,
    nor shall, but to be curst;
And oh! that I (fond I) should first
    of any lover
This truth at my own charge to other fools discover!

2.
You that have promis'd to your selves
    propriety in love,
Know womens hearts like straw do move,
    and what we call
Their sympathy, is but love to jett in general.

3.
All mankind are alike to them;
    and, though we iron find
That never with a Loadstone joyn'd,
    'tis not its fault,
It is because near the loadstone yet was never brought.

4.
If where a gentle Bee hath fall'n
    and laboured to his power,
A new succeeds not to that Flower,
    but passes by,
'Tis to be thought, the gallant else-where loads his thigh.

5.
For still the flowers ready stand:
    one buzzes round about,
One lights, one tasts, gets in, gets out;
    all, all waies use them,
Till all their sweets are gone, and all again refuse them.

[Loves Clock]

1.
That none beguiled be by times quick flowing,
Lovers have in their hearts a clock still going;
   For, though time be nimble, his motions
        are quicker
        and thicker
   Where Love hath his notions:

2.
Hope is the main spring on which moves desire,
And these do the lesse wheels, fear, joy, inspire;
   The ballance is thought, evermore
        clicking
        and striking,
   And ne're giving ore.

3.
Occasion's the hand which still's moving round,
Till by it the Critical hour may be found,
   And when that falls out, it will strike
        kisses,
        strange blisses,
   And what you best like.

[Song. "No, no, faire heretique"]

1

No, no, fair Heretique, it needs must bee
      But an ill love in mee,
      And worse for thee.
For were it in my Power,
To love thee now this hower,
      More than I did the last;
'Twould then so fall,
I might not Love at all;
    Love that can flow, and can admit increase,
    Admits as well an ebb, and may grow lesse.

2

True love is still the same: the torrid Zones,
      And those more frigid ones,
      It must not know:
For Love growne cold or hot,
Is Lust, or Friendship, not
      The thing wee have;
For that's a flame would die,
Held downe, or up too high:
    Then thinke I love more than I can expresse,
    And would love more, could I but love thee lesse.

[Song.
"Why so pale and wan fond Lover?"]

1.

Why so pale and wan, fond Lover?
    Prithee, why so pale?
Will, when looking well can't move her,
    Looking ill prevaile?
    Prithee, why so pale?

2.

Why so dull and mute, young Sinner?
    Prithee, why so mute?
Will, when speaking well can't win her,
    Saying nothing doo't?
    Prithee, why so mute?

3.

Quit, quit, for shame, this will not move,
    This cannot take her;
If of her selfe she will not Love,
    Nothing can make her,
    The Devill take her!

[Loves Siege]

1.
'Tis now since I sate down before
    That foolish Fort, a heart,
(Time strangely spent) a Year, and more,
    And still I did my part:

2.
Made my approaches, from her hand
    Unto her lip did rise,
And did already understand
    The language of her eyes;

3.
Proceeded on with no lesse Art,
    My Tongue was Engineer:
I thought to undermine the heart
    By whispering in the ear.

4.
When this did nothing, I brought down
    Great Canon-oaths, and shot
A thousand thousand to the Town,
    And still it yeelded not.

5.
I then resolv'd to starve the place
    By cutting off all kisses,
Praysing and gazing on her face,
    And all such little blisses.

6.
To draw her out, and from her strength,
    I drew all batteries in:
And brought my self to lie at length
    As if no siege had been.

7.

When I had done what man could do,
    And thought the place mine owne,
The Enemy lay quiet too,
    And smil'd at all was done.

8.

I sent to know from whence, and where,
    These hopes, and this relief?
A Spie inform'd, Honour was there,
    And did command in chief.

9.

March, march, (quoth I) the word straight give,
    Let's lose no time, but leave her:
That giant upon ayre will live,
    And hold it out for ever.

10.

To such a place our Camp remove
    As will no siege abide;
I hate a fool that starves her Love
    Onely to feed her pride.

Farewel to Love

1.
Well shadow'd Landskip, fare-ye-well:
How I have lov'd you, none can tell,
    At least so well
  As he that now hates more
  Than e're he lov'd before.

2.
But, my dear nothings, take your leave,
No longer must you me deceive,
    Since I perceive
  All the deceit, and know
  Whence the mistake did grow.

3.
As he, whose quicker eye doth trace
A false star shot to a mark't place,
    Do's run apace,
  And thinking it to catch,
  A gelly up do's snatch:

4.
So our dull souls, tasting delight
Far off, by sence, and appetite,
    Think that is right
  And real good; when yet
  'Tis but the Counterfeit.

5.
Oh! how I glory now! that I
Have made this new discovery!
    Each wanton eye
  Enflam'd before: no more
  Will I encrease that score.

6.
If I gaze now, 'tis but to see
What manner of deaths-head 'twill be,
    When it is free
      From that fresh upper skin,
      The gazers Joy, and sin.

7.
The Gum and glist'ning which with art
And studied method in each part
    Hangs down the heart,
      Looks (just) as if, that day,
      Snails there had crawl'd the *Hay*.

8.
The Locks, that curl'd o're each eare be,
Hang like two Master-worms to me,
    That (as we see)
      Have tasted to the rest
      Two holes, where they lik't best.

9.
A quick corse me-thinks I spy
In every woman; and mine eye,
    At passing by,
      Checks, and is troubled, just
      As if it rose from Dust.

10.
They mortifie, not heighten me:
These of my sins the Glasses be:
    And here I see
      How I have lov'd before.
      And so I love no more.

Upon two Sisters

Beleev't yong Man, I can as eas'ly tell
How many yards and inches 'tis to hell;
Unriddle all predestination,
Or the nice points we now dispute upon!
Had the three goddesses been just as fair,
[. . . . .]
It had not been so easily decided,
And sure the apple must have been divided:
It must, it must; hee's impudent, dares say
Which is the handsomer till one's away.
And it was necessary it should be so;
While Nature did foresee it, and did know
When she had fram'd the Eldest, that each heart
Must at the first sight feel the blind-god's dart:
And sure as can be, had she made but one,
No plague had been more sure destruction;
For we had lik't, lov'd, burnt to ashes too,
In half the time that we are chusing now.
Variety and equal objects make
The busie eye still doubtful which to take:
This lip, this hand, this foot, this eye, this face,
The others body, gesture, or her grace;
And whilst we thus dispute which of the two,
We unresolv'd go out, and nothing do.
He sure is happy'st that has hopes of either,
Next him is he that sees them both together.

[A Summons to Town]

Sir,
Whether these lines do find you out,
Putting or clearing of a doubt;
Whether Predestination,
Or reconciling three in one,
Or the unriddling how men die,
And live at once eternally,
Now take you up, know 'tis decreed
You straight bestride the Colledge Steed:
Leave *Socinus* and the Schoolmen
(Which *Jack Bond* swears do but fool men),
And come to Town; 'tis fit you show
Your self abroad, that men may know
(What e're some learned men have guest)
That Oracles are not yet ceas't:
There you shall find the wit, and wine
Flowing alike, and both divine;
Dishes, with names not known in books,
And less amongst the Colledge-Cooks,
With sauce so pregnant that you need
Not stay till hunger bids you feed.
The sweat of learned *Johnsons* brain,
And gentle *Shakespear*'s eas'er strain,
A hackney-coach conveys you to,
In spite of all that rain can do:
And for your eighteen pence you sit
The Lord and Judge of all fresh wit.
News in one day as much w'have here,
As serves all *Windsor* for a year,
And which the Carrier brings to you,
After 't has here been found not true.
Then think what Company's design'd
To meet you here, men so refin'd,
Their very common talk at boord,
Makes wise, or mad a young Court-Lord,

And makes him capable to be
Umpire in's Fathers Company.
Where no disputes, nor forc't defence
Of a mans person for his sence
Take up the time, all strive to be
Masters of truth, as victory:
And where you come, I'de boldly swear
A Synod might as eas'ly erre.

[The Wits]
(A Sessions of the Poets)

1.

A Sessions was held the other day,
And *Apollo* himself was at it (they say;)
The Laurel that had been so long reserv'd,
Was now to be given to him best deserv'd.
        And
Therefore the wits of the Town came thither,
'Twas strange to see how they flocked together;
Each strongly confident of his own way,
Thought to gain the Laurel away that day.

2.

There was *Selden*, and he sate hard by the chair;
Wenman not far off, which was very fair;
Sands with *Townsend*, for they kept no order;
Digby and *Chillingworth* a little further:
        And
There was *Lucans* translator too, and he
That makes God speak so bigge in's Poetry;
Selwin and *Waller*, and *Berkeleys* both the brothers;
Jack Vaughan and *Porter*, with divers others.

3.

The first that broke silence was good old *Ben*,
Prepar'd before with Canary wine,
And he told them plainly he deserv'd the Bayes,
For his were call'd Works, where others were but Plaies,
        And
Bid them remember how he had purg'd the Stage
Of errors, that had lasted many an Age,
And he hop'd they did not think the *silent Woman*,
The Fox and the *Alchymist* out done by no man.

4.

Apollo stopt him there, and bid him not go on,
'Twas merit, he said, and not presumption
Must carry it; at which *Ben* turned about,
And in great choler offer'd to go out:
        But
Those that were there thought it not fit
To discontent so ancient a wit;
And therefore *Apollo* call'd him back agen,
And made him mine host of his own new Inne.

5.

Tom Carew was next, but he had a fault
That would not well stand with a Laureat;
His Muse was hard bound, and th'issue of's brain
Was seldom brought forth but with trouble and pain.
        And
All that were present there did agree,
A Laureats Muse should be easie and free;
Yet sure 'twas not that, but 'twas thought that his Grace
Consider'd, he was well he had a Cup-bearers place.

6.

Will. Davenant, asham'd of a foolish mischance
That he had got lately travelling in *France*,
Modestly hoped the handsomeness of 's Muse
Might any deformity about him excuse.
        And
Surely the Company would have been content,
If they could have found any President;
But in all their Records either in Verse or Prose,
There was not one Laureat without a nose.

7.

To *Will Berkeley* sure all the wits meant well,
But first they would see how his snow would sell:
Will smil'd and swore in their judgements they went lesse,

That concluded of merit upon successe.
               So
Suddenly taking his place agen,
He gave way to *Selwin*, that streight stept in;
But, alas! he had been so lately a wit,
That *Apollo* himself hardly knew him yet.

               8.

Toby Mathew (pox on 't! how came he there?)
Was busily whispering some-body i'th'ear,
When he had the honour to be nam'd i'th Court:
But Sir, you may thank my Lady *Carlile* for't:
               For
Had not her Character furnisht you out
With something of handsome, without all doubt
You and your sorry Lady Muse had been
In the number of those that were not to come in.

               9.

In haste two or three from the court came in,
And they brought letters (forsooth) from the Queen;
'Twas discreetly done too, for if they had come
Without them, they had scarce been let into the room.
               This
Made a dispute; for 'twas plain to be seen
Each man had a mind to gratify the Queen:
But *Apollo* himself could not think it fit;
There was difference, he said, 'twixt fooling and wit.

              10.

Suckling next was call'd, but did not appear,
And strait one whisperd *Apollo* in's ear.
That of all men living he cared not for't,
He loved not the Muses so well as his sport;
               And
Prized black eyes, or a lucky hit
At bowls, above all the Trophies of wit;

But *Apollo* was angry, and publiquely said,
'Twere fit that a fine were set on his head.

11.

Wat Montague now stood forth to his tryal,
And did not so much as suspect a denial;
Wise *Apollo* then asked him first of all,
If he understood his own Pastoral.
        For
If he could do it, 'twould plainly appear,
He understood more than any man there,
And did merit the Bayes above all the rest,
But the Mounsier was modest, and silence confest.

12.

During these troubles, in the Crowd was hid
One that *Apollo* soon mist, little *Sid*;
And having spied him, call'd him out of the throng,
And advis'd him in his ear not to write so strong.
        Then
Murrey was summon'd, but 'twas urg'd that he
Was Chief already of another Company.

13.

Hales set by himself most gravely did smile
To see them about nothing keep such a coil;
Apollo had spied him, but knowing his mind
Past by, and call'd *Faulkland* that sate just behind:
        But
He was of late so gone with Divinity,
That he had almost forgot his Poetry,
Though to say the truth (and *Apollo* did know it)
He might have been both his Priest and his Poet.

14.

At length who but an Alderman did appear,
At which *Will. Davenant* began to swear;

But wiser *Apollo* bade him draw nigher,
And when he was mounted a little higher
             He
Openly declared that 'twas the best signe
Of good store of wit to have good store of coyn,
And without a Syllable more or lesse said,
He put the Laurel on the Aldermans head.

15.

At this all the wits were in such a maze
That for a good while they did nothing but gaze
One upon another, not a man in the place
But had discontent writ in great in his face.
             Onely
The small Poets clear'd up again,
Out of hope (as 'twas thought) of borrowing;
But sure they were out, for he forfeits his Crown,
When he lends to any Poet about the Town.

To his much honoured
the Lord Lepington, upon his translation of
Malvezzi, his 'Romulus' and 'Tarquin'

It is so rare and new a thing to see
Ought that belongs to young Nobility
In print, but their owne clothes, that we must praise
You as we would doe those first shew the wayes
To Arts or to new Worlds: You have begun:
Taught travell'd youth what 'tis it should have done:
For't has indeed too strong a custome bin
To carry out more wit than we bring in.
You have done otherwise, brought home (my Lord)
The choicest things fam'd Countreyes doe afford:
Malvezzi by your meanes is English growne,
And speaks our tongue as well now as his owne.
Malvezzi, he: whom 'tis as hard to praise
To merit, as to imitate his wayes.
He does not show us *Rome* great suddenly,
As if the Empire were a Tympany,
But gives it naturall growth, tels how, and why
The little body grew so large and high;
Describes each thing so lively, that we are
Concern'd our selves before we are aware:
And at the warres they and their neighbours wag'd
Each man is present still, and still engag'd.
Like a good prospective he strangely brings
Things distant to us: and in these two Kings
We see what made greatnesse. And what 't has been
Made that greatnesse contemptible againe.
And all this not tediously deriv'd,
But like to Worlds in little Maps contriv'd.
'Tis he that doth the Roman Dame restore,
Makes *Lucrece* chaster for her being whore;
Gives her a kind Revenge for *Tarquins* sinne,
For ravish't first, she ravisheth againe.
She sayes such fine things after't, that we must

In spite of vertue thanke foule Rape and Lust,
Since 'twas the cause no woman would have had,
Though she's of *Lucrece* side, *Tarquin* lesse bad.
    But stay: like one that thinks to bring his friend
A mile or two, and sees the journeyes end,
I straggle on too farre; long graces do
But keepe good stomacks off that would fall to.

To my Friend Will. Davenant upon his Poem of Madagascar

What mighty Princes Poets are! those things
   The great ones stick at, and our very Kings
Lay downe, they venter on; and with great ease,
Discover, conquer, what, and where they please.
Some Flegmatick Sea-Captaine would have staid
For money now, or Victualls; not have waid
Anchor without 'em; Thou (*Will*) do'st not stay
So much as for a Wind, but go'st away,
Land'st, View'st, the Country; fight'st, puts't all to rout,
Before another cou'd be putting out!
And now the newes in towne is, *Dav'nant's* come
From *Madagascar*, Fraught with Laurell home,
And welcome (*Will*) for the first time, but prithee
In thy next Voyage, bring the Gold too with thee.

(To my Friend Will. Davenant,) On his other Poems

Thou hast redeemed us, *Will*; and future Times
   Shall not account unto the Age's crimes
Dearth of pure Wit: since the great Lord of it
(*Donne*) parted hence, no Man has ever writ
So neere him in's owne way: I would commend
Particulars, but then, how should I end
Without a Volume? Ev'ry line of thine
Would ask (to praise it right) Twenty of mine.

An Answer to some Verses made in his Praise

The antient Poets and their learned rimes,
We still admire in these our later times,
And celebrate their fames: Thus, though they die,
Their names can never taste mortalitie:
Blind *Homer's* Muse and *Virgil's* stately Verse,
While any live, shall never need a herse.
Since then to these such praise was justly due
For what they did, what shall be said to you?
These had their helps; they writ of Gods and Kings,
Of Temples, Battels, and such gallant things:
But you of Nothing; how could you have writ,
Had you but chose a Subject to your Wit?
To praise *Achilles*, or the Trojan crew,
Shewed little art, for praise was but their due.
To say she's fair that's fair, this is no pains:
He shews himself most Poet, that most feigns:
To find out vertues strangely hid in me,
I, there's the art and learned Poetrie;
To make one striding of a Barbed Steed,
Prancing a stately round: (I use indeed
To ride *Bat Jewels* Jade;) this is the skill,
This shews the Poet wants not wit at will.
 I must admire aloof, and for my part
 Be well contented, since you do't with art.

A Ballade
Upon a Wedding

1.

I tell thee *Dick*, where I have been,
Where I the rarest things have seen,
  Oh things without compare!
Such sights again cannot be found
In any place on English ground,
  Be it at Wake, or Fair.

2.

At *Charing-Cross*e, hard by the way
Where we (thou know'st) do sell our Hay,
  There is a house with stairs;
And there did I see comming down
Such folk as are not in our Town,
  Forty at least, in Pairs.

3.

Amongst the rest, one Pest'lent fine,
(His beard no bigger though then thine)
  Walkt on before the rest:
Our Landlord looks like nothing to him:
The King, (God blesse him) 'twould undo him,
  Should he go still so drest.

4.

At Course-a-Park, without all doubt,
He should have first been taken out
  By all the maids i'th' Town:
Though lusty *Roger* there had been,
Or little *George* upon the Green,
  Or *Vincent* of the Crown.

5.

But wot you what? the youth was going
To make an end of all his woing;
   The Parson for him staid:
Yet by his leave (for all his haste)
He did not wish so much all past,
   (Perchance) as did the maid.

6.

The maid, (and thereby hangs a tale,
For such a maid no Whitson-ale
   Could ever yet produce)
No Grape that's kindly ripe, could be
So round, so plump, so soft as she,
   Nor half so full of Juyce.

7.

Her finger was so small, the Ring
Would not stay on which they did bring,
   It was too wide a Peck:
And to say truth (for out it must)
It lookt like the great Collar (just)
   About our young Colts neck.

8.

Her feet beneath her Petticoat,
Like little mice stole in and out,
   As if they fear'd the light:
But oh! she dances such a way!
No Sun upon an Easter day
   Is half so fine a sight.

9.

He would have kist her once or twice,
But she would not, she was so nice,
   She would not do't in sight;
And then she lookt as who should say

I will do what I list to day,
        And you shall do't at night.

        10.

Her Cheeks so rare a white was on,
No Dazy makes comparison
        (Who sees them is undone)
For streaks of red were mingled there,
Such as are on a Katherine Pear,
        (The side that's next the Sun).

        11.

Her mouth so small when she doth speak,
Thou'dst swear her teeth her words did break,
        That they might passage get;
But she so handles still the matter,
They came as good as ours, or better,
        And are not spoil'd one whit.

        12.

Her lips were red; and one was thin,
Compar'd to that was next her chin;
        (Some Bee had stung it newly.)
But (*Dick*) her eyes so guard her face;
I durst no more upon her gaze,
        Than on the Sun in *July*.

        13.

If wishing should be any sin,
The Parson self had guilty bin,
        (She lookt that day so purely;)
And did the youth so oft the feat
At night, as some did in conceit,
        It would have spoil'd him surely.

14.
Passion oh me! how I run on!
There's that that would be thought upon,
      (I trow) besides the Bride:
The bus'nesse of the Kitchin great;
For it is fit that mean should eat,
      Nor was it there deni'd.

15.
Just in the nick the Cook knockt thrice,
And all the waiters in a trice
      His summons did obey:
Each serving-man with dish in hand,
Marcht boldly up, like our Train Band,
      Presented, and away.

16.
When all meat was on the Table,
What man of knife, or teeth, was able
      To stay to be intreated?
And this the very reason was,
Before the Parson could say Grace,
      The Company was seated.

17.
Now hatts fly off, and youths carrouse;
Healths first go round, and then the house,
      The Brides came thick and thick:
And, when 'twas nam'd anothers health,
Perhaps he made it hers by stealth.
      (And who could help it? *Dick*)

18.
O'th' sodain up they rise and dance,
Then sit again and sigh, and glance;
      Then dance again and kisse:
Thus sev'ral waies the time did passe,

Whilst ev'ry Woman wisht her place,
      And ev'ry man wisht his.

      19.

By this time all were stoln aside
To counsel and undresse the Bride;
      But that he must not know:
But yet 'twas thought he ghest her mind,
And did not mean to stay behind
      Above an hour or so.

      20.

When in he came (*Dick*) there she lay
Like new-faln snow melting away;
      ('Twas time I trow to part)
Kisses were now the onely stay,
Which soon she gave, as who should say,
      God b'w'y'! with all my heart.

      21.

But just as Heav'ns would have to crosse it,
In came the Bridesmaids with the Posset:
      The Bridegroom ate in spight;
For had he left the Women to't,
It would have cost two hours to do't,
      Which were too much that night.

      22.

At length the candles out, and now
All that they had not done, they do:
      What that is, who can tell?
But I believe it was no more
Than thou and I have done before
      With *Bridget*, and with *Nell*.

On New-years Day 1640
To the King

1.

Awake (great sir) the Sun shines here,
   Gives all Your Subjects a New-yeer,
Onely we stay till You appear,
For thus by us Your Power is understood:
He may make fair days, You must make them good.
     Awake, awake,
      and take
   Such Presents as poor men can make,
   They can adde little unto blisse
     who cannot wish.

2.

May no ill vapour cloud the skie,
Bold storms invade the Soveraigntie,
But gales of joy, so fresh, so high,
That You may think Heav'n sent to try this year
What sayl, or burthen, a Kings mind could bear.
     Awake, awake, etc

3.

May all the discords in Your State
(Like those in Musick we create)
Be govern'd at so wise a rate,
That what would of it self sound harsh, or fright,
May be so temper'd that it may delight.
     Awake, awake, etc.

4.

What conquerors from battels find,
Or lovers when their Doves are kind,
Take up henceforth our Masters mind,
Make such strange Rapes upon the place, 't may be
No longer joy there, but an extasie.
     Awake, awake, etc.

5.
May every pleasure and delight,
That has, or does, your sence invite,
Double this year, save those o'th' night:
For such a Marriage-bed must know no more
Than repetition of what was before.
    Awake, awake,
    And take
Such Presents as poor men can make,
They can add little unto blisse
    who cannot wish.

Upon my Lord Brohall's Wedding

Dialogue

S[uckling]   B[ond]'

S.   In bed, dull man?
When *Love* and *Hymens* revels are begun,
And the Church Ceremonies past and done?

B.   Why, who's gone mad to-day?

S.   Dull Heretick, thou wouldst say,
He that is gone to heaven's gone astray;
   Brohall our gallant friend
Is gone to Church, as Martyrs to the fire.

B.   Who marry differ i'th' end,
      Since both do take
The hardest way to what they most desire.

S. Nor staid he till the formal Priest had done,
But ere that part was finisht, his begun.

B.   Which did reveal
The haste and eagernesse men have to seal
   That long to tell the money.

S. A sprig of willow in his hat he wore,—

B. The loosers badge and liv'ry heretofore,

S. But now so ordered, that it might be taken
By lookers on, forsaking as forsaken.
      And now and then
A carelesse smile broke forth, which spoke his mind,—

B. And seem'd to say she might have been more kind.

S.   When this (dear *Jack*) I saw,
           Thought I,
        How weak is Lovers Law?

B. The bonds made there (like gypsies knots) with ease
   Are fast and loose, as they that hold them please.

S. But was the fair Nymphs praise or power lesse,
   That led him captive now to happinesse,
   'Cause she did not a forreign aid despise.
   But enter'd breaches made by others' eyes?
        The gods forbid!
   There must be some to shoot and batter down,
   Others to force and to take in the Town.
        To Hawkes (good *Jack*) and hearts
          There may
        Be sev'ral waies and Arts:
   One watches them perchance, and makes them tame;
   Another, when they're ready, shows them game.

Juvenilia and Seasonal Works

Upon St. Thomas his unbeliefe

Faith comes by heare-say, love by sight: then hee
May well beleive, and love whom hee doth see:
But since men leave both hope, and charitie,
And faith is made the greatest of the three,
All doctrine goes for truth: then say I thus,
More goes to heaven with *Thomas Didymus*.

Upon Christmas Eve

Vaile cobwebs from the white-ned floore
And let *Arachne* spin noe more;
With holly-bushes all adorne
Untill the comeing of the morne,
And fancy then the Lord of Light is there
As he did once in *Moses*-bush appeare.

Upon Christ his birth

Strange news! a Cittie full? will none give way
To lodge a guest that comes not every day?
Noe inne, nor taverne void? yet I descry
One empty place alone, where wee may ly:
In too much fullnesse is some want: but where?
Mens empty hearts: let's aske for lodging there,
But if they not admit us, then wee'le say
Their hearts, as well as inn's, are made of clay.

Upon Stephen stoned

Under this heape of stones interred lies
    No holocaust, but stoned sacrifice
Burnt not by altar-coales, but by the fire
        Of Jewish ire,
Whose softest wordes in their hard hearts alone
        Congeal'd to stone,
Nor peirceing them recoild in him againe,
        Whoe beeing slaine
As not forgetfull, whence they once did come,
Now being stones hee found in them a tombe.

Upon St Johns-day comeing after Christmas day

Let the Divines dispute the case, and try
    The dubiousness of that great mystery
That *John* should live untill the day of doome:
This may sufffice, he stayes till *Christ* is come.

Upon Innocents day

What reason can there in an infant lurke?
    Or in an innocent what hurtfull worke?
Yet must you, suckeing infants, dy for these,
White as your milke who have your consciences?
Noe 'tis not strange: soe should all martyres dy
Drinkeing the new-milk of sincerity.

Upon Newyeares day

Arise my Muse, a Newyear's-gift præpare,
Noe thing of too much cost, nor yet soe rare,
But fitt for Ladyes dresses, and rehearse
A Pedlar's pack of fancy's in thy verse,
That if thy fancies have a prosperous fate
They may with favours thee retaliate.

Upon the Epiphanie
Or starr that appear'd to the wisemen

Astrologers, from hence you may devise
Peripatetick orders in the skies:
Sith here a Philosophick wakeing starr
Hath taught the Magi comeing from afarr
The *summum bonum* in a trice to find
Not in high roofes, but oxen-stalls inshrin'd.
O calculate this starr, and surely then
You'l find it does præsage good health to men.

Upon Christmas

Haile wellcome time, whoes long expected date
The proner hearts of men doth elevate
Who from their toile cessations now require,
And live in warme *Elysiums* by the fire
Upon whoes sunny bank's they take delight
To see the winged, and foure-footed fight,
And charge each other in the flameing field's
With spitts for speares, and dripping-pans for sheilds;
Some better friends doe turne about, and play
Till scorcht with heat become to men a prey.

And schollers too, from prison-schoole set free
Proclaime aloud a gaole deliverie,
Invoke the Gods of sports, nor feare the maine
By Plough-day writs to bee attach't againe.
Well did our fathers then by *Christ* set free
Elect us thus to their fraternitie!
But shall those impious mouth's by new-fond lights
Inspir'd revile, and loath these sacred rites,
Whoes festivalls with prayer, and almes allay'd,
A time of Charitie, and gladnesse made,
Shall they with poison-beareing slaunder staine
This time, and it abolish as profane?
Noe Noe: let's keepe it still whilst them wee see
With Christmas pull downe *Christ* Nativitie.

[Faith and Doubt]

That *Heaven* should visit *Earth* and come to see
Poore wretched *Man*, rich but in Miserie,
That *Hee* whom all the *Heavens* could not contayne
Should in a Virgin-wombe soe long remayne,
Is such a wonder and soe great! that heere
Our *Faith* not *Reason* must us steere.
But that the *God* of Life, should come to dy
And dye for us, O there's the howe, and why!
Each *Man* is *Thomas* heere, and faine would see
Something to helpe his Infidellitie,
But I beleive; *Lord* helpe my faithlesse mynd
And with Sainct *Thomas* lett mee Pardon find.

A Dreame

Scarce had I slept my wonted rownd
  But that meethoughts I heard the last *Trompe* sownd:
And in a Moment *Earth's* faire *Frame* did passe,
The *Heav'ns* did melt, and all confus'on was.
My thoughts straight gave mee, *Earth's* great daie was come,
And that I was nowe to receive my doome.
'Twixt Hope and Feare, whil'st I thus trembling stood
Feareing the Bad, and yet expecting Good:
Summon'd I was, to showe howe I had spent,
That span-long tyme which *God* on earth mee lent.
Cold Feares possest mee; for I knewe noe Lyes
(Though guilded o're) could blynd th' Eternall's Eyes.
Besides my Bosome frend my Conscience mee accus'd,
That I too much this little Tyme abus'd.
And nowe noe summes of gould, noe bribes (alasse)
Could mee repreive, Sentence must straight waie passe.
Great Frends could nothing doe, noe lustfull Peere,
Noe smooth-fac'd *Buckingham*, was *Favourite* heere.
Theis helpes were vaine; what could I then saie more?
I had done ill, and death lay at the dore.
But yet meethoughts it was too much to dy,
To die a while, much lesse eternally;
And therefore streight I did my Sinnes unmaske
And in *Christ's* name, a *Pardon* there did aske
Which *God* then granted; and *God* grant hee may
Make this my dreame proove true i'th' later day.

Explanatory Notes

p.12. *A Supplement...* the first nine lines supposedly come from Shakespeare's *Lucrece* (ll. 386–395), but are here substantially different from the version of the Shakespeare poem that we have today. Whether Suckling was working from a corrupt source, or from a different version of the poem is unclear.

p.15 *Barley-break* is a rural game in which two couples, positioned at opposite ends of a field, try to exchange partners while not being caught by a third couple positioned in the centre of the field; the latter zone was known as *Hell* (or *prison*). If the Hell-dwellers caught one of the other couples, then they exchanged places. References to this game abound in poetry of the late 16th and early 17th centuries.

p.19 A Barber:
— *great* Swedens *force*: King Gustavus Adolphus, d. 1632.
— *Witel*: Whitehall
— *Burse*: *bourse*, or exchange.

p.24 *Metamorphosis*. The poem uses a number of famous scenes from Ovid's *Metamorphoses*.
— *Io / cow*: Io was a mortal woman, and a priestess of the Goddess Hera in Argos. She came to the notice of Zeus (i.e. Jupiter / Jove), who lusted after her. There are various versions of the tale, but the essence of it is that she rejected Zeus' advances, and then Zeus turned her into a heifer in order to hide her from his wife (while some other versions have the jealous Hera doing this).
— *Narcissus*: According to *Metamorphoses*, Book III, Narcissus's mother was told by the Tiresias that he would have a long life, provided he never recognized himself. However, his rejection of the love of the nymph Echo attracted the vengeance of the gods. He fell in love with his own reflection in the waters of a spring and pined away; the flower that bears his name sprang up where he died. Pausanias, in *Description of Greece*, Book IX, said however that it was more likely that Narcissus, consoling himself for the death of his beloved twin sister, his exact counterpart, sat gazing into the spring in order to recall her face.
— *Jove / Golden rain*: the appearance of Jupiter (Jove) to Danaë –

another who caught Zeus' fancy – in her bedroom as a shower of golden rain.

p.25 *Lutea Allison*: a Roman fort (now called Liesborn) near the town of Wesel, which in Suckling's time was in the Spanish Netherlands, but is today in Germany. Suckling mentioned the town in a letter written in 1630, and may have visited it during his time in the Netherlands. Lutea presumably comes from Latin *lutum*, *clay* or *mud*, thus indicating an earthwork fortress.

— *Si sola es, nulla es* (Latin): *lit.* "It is alone, it is nothing", although Line 14 paraphrases this in more poetic fashion.

— *Diana*: huntress goddess, Roman equivalent of the Greek goddess, Aphrodite.

— *Hymen*: god of marriage.

p.26 *Lady Seimor*: Probably Katherine, wife of Francis Seymour, first Baron of Trowbridge, whose father's estate was close to that of the Earl of Middlesex's at Milcote, which Suckling frequently visited.

p.26 *Non est mortale quod opto* (Latin): from Ovid's *Metamorphoses*, ii. 55, slightly reworked. "You wish for that which no mortal may seek." In the original, the phrase is uttered by Helios, rebuking Phaeton.

p.27. *Sir John Laurence* = Sir John Lawrence, an engineer who arranged for running water to be supplied from a nearby stream to Wiston House in 1630.

— *Lord Middlesex / Wiston*: Lord Middlesex owned the house at Wiston, Sussex, until 1634. The house was originally built in 1576.

p.29. *Lady E.C.* may be Elizabeth Cranfield, cousin to Suckling, who married Lord Sheffield in 1631.

p.31. *Lady Carlile*: Lucy Hay, Countess of Carlisle (1599–1660), a great beauty of the day, and much admired by courtiers such as Suckling and Thomas Carew (the author's companion here). She also features in poems by Carew and Herrick, among others. The original published version of this poem lacks the final stanza ascribed to J.S. One can understand why a careful editor, or typesetter, might have wished to avoid blame for it.

p.33. *T.C. having the P.*: T.C. is Thomas Carew; the P is the Pox, or venereal disease.

— *the French*: a pun, in that the pox was often referred to as "the French disease".

p.36. *Lady Middlesex*: see note for p.27 above.

p.41. *Mr Davenant*: William Davenant (1606–1668) was a close friend of Suckling's, and was named poet laureate in succession to Jonson in 1638. There were persistent rumours that Davenant was the illegitimate son of Shakespeare, but it is more likely that these were prompted by Davenant himself. He was knighted in 1643 after his involvement in the siege of Gloucester.

— *Persinda*: there is a *Persinde* mentioned in *Faramond, ou l'histoire de France*, Part V (registered 1658, published 1662) by Gaultier de Costes de La Calprenède (1609–1663). Publication therefore occurred *after* Suckling's death, but it remains possible that manuscript versions were in circulation earlier, as several of his books were published during Suckling's lifetime.

p.48 *Coridon*: a generic name for a participant (usually a shepherd) in a Pastoral. The speaker with this name is here (unusually) female.

p.50. *Sonnet*: in the usage of the time a *Sonnet* was a little song, and was not obliged to be a 14-line poem.

p.52 *chaplets* = garlands, or circlets about the head.

— *Sophonisba*: a Carthaginian noblewoman who lived during the Second Punic War, and the daughter of Hasdrubal Gisco Gisgonis. In an act that echoed down the ages, she poisoned herself rather than be humiliated in a Roman triumph.

— *Philoclea*: a character in Book I of the *Countess of Pembroke's Arcadia* (written by Sir Philip Sidney in the 1570s, but only published in 1590, after his death, by his sister, the Countess). The Duke of Arcadia, Basilius, journeys to the oracle at Delphi and receives a bleak prediction: his daughters will be stolen by undesirable suitors, he will be cuckolded by his wife, and his throne will be usurped by a foreigners. Hoping to prevent this, Basilius entrusts the government of Arcadia to the loyal Philanax, and retires to a lodge in the country with his wife, Gynecia, their attractive daughters, Pamela and Philoclea, his servant, Dametas, and the latter's wife and daughter, Miso and Mopsa. In a nearby city, Pyrocles and Musidorus pass the night; they are cousins, princes, and best friends, and are famous throughout Greece for their heroic exploits. Pyrocles, upon seeing a picture of Philoclea at a gallery, is overwhelmed by a passionate desire to see her in person. Pyrocles disguises himself as Cleophila, an Amazonian lady," and heads for Basilius's country home, accompanied by Musidorus. Deceived by Cleophila's feminine disguise, Basilius falls in love with her, and invites her to stay with the family. While Musidorus covertly observes this meeting, he is overwhelmed by a passionate love for the elder daughter, Pamela, and decides to disguise himself as a shepherd, Dorus, in order to gain access to her. When everyone congregates in an arbor to hear the shepherds sing, a lion and bear attack the party. Cleophila kills the lion, saving Philoclea; Dorus kills the bear, saving Pamela. Cleophila's derring-do leads Gynecia to suspect her secret male sex, while Philoclea forms an intense "sisterly" affection for Cleophila.

— *Pirocles* = Pyrocles (see above).

— *Amphialus*: the story of the rebel Amphialus is from the revised *Arcadia*, written later than the episode referred to above. Amphialus is the nephew of Basilius. He was heir to the throne of Arcadia before the birth of Pamela. He loves Philoclea. He causes the deaths of, or kills, Philoxenus, Timotheus, Argalus, Parthenia, and Cecropia. Tries to commit suicide. He is loved by Helen.

p.57 *Desdain*: original poem from *Les Satyres du Sr Regnier* (1614).

p.61 *Sir Toby Mathew*: another of the "Wits" and pilloried (good-naturedly) in Suckling's 'Sessions of the Poets' (see note to p.77).

p.62 *Black-Friars*: An area of London between the Thames and Ludgate Hill, whose name derives from the priory founded in the area by Dominican monks in the 13th century. In Suckling's day there was a Blackfriars Theatre in the area, more or less opposite the Globe, on the other bank of the river.

— *old Whitehall*: Whitehall Palace, which burned down in 1698, was a favourite palace of King Henry VIII, where he married two of his wives, as well as being home to King Charles I, who kept his art collection there.

p.66 *loadstone*: = lodestone, a mineral that acts as a magnet. Often used in amulets and talismans in Suckling's day.

p.67 *jett* = jet: a black semi-precious stone.

p.75 *A Summons*
— *Socinus*: Fausto Sozzini (Faustus Socinus in Latin, 1539–1604), theologian and founder of Socinianism, which was an early version of Christian unitarianism, whereby the concept of the Trinity is denied. Anti-trinitarian beliefs were much in the air during the first century after the Reformation.
— *Schoolmen*: university theologians.
— *Jack Bond*: identity unclear, but there is a letter from Suckling to a "Jack", and Clayton (editor of the 1971 Oxford Standard Authors edition of Suckling's work) observes that a Mrs Bond, wife of one Thomas Bond (and perhaps mother to Jack?), was a source of information for John Aubrey's information on Suckling in his *Brief Lives*.
— *Johnson* = Ben Jonson (1572–1637), poet, playwright, and poet laureate of England.

p.77 *The Wits / A Sessions*: The 'Sessions' title is unlikely to be authorial. 'The Wits' may also be a deliberate echo of Davenant's play of that name which was performed in 1636, the year before this poem was written.
— *Selden*: John Selden (1584–1654), lawyer and scholar. John Milton referred to him in 1644 as "the chief of learned men reputed in this land." His published works include writings (in Latin) on Judaism and Jewish law, and Semitic mythology. He was also an important historian.
— *Wenman*: Sir Frances Wenman (1597?–after 1640), son of Sir Richard, first Viscount Wenman.
— *Sands*: George Sandys (1578–1644)
— *Townsend*: Aurelian Townshend (1601?–1643?): poet and playwright; close friend of Thomas Carew. He composed a masque in which the Queen performed at Court and worked closely with Inigo Jones on a number of productions. He experienced a rapid fall from grace – the reasons for which are unclear – and, by 1643, was seeking protection from his creditors.

— *Digby*: Sir Kenelm Digby (1603–1665), courtier and diplomat, and author of philosophical treatises. A significant figure in intellectual circles at the time, he was hampered somewhat by his professed Catholicism.
— *Chillingworth*: William Chillingworth (1602-1644), godson of Archbishop Laud and a controversial clergyman in his own right. He switched sides, doctrinally, on two occasions, finally settling as an Anglican, and composing *The Religion of Protestants a Safe Way to Salvation*, published in 1637.
— *Lucans translator* = Thomas May (1595–1650). He published a number of translations (including Virgil and Martial) and also wrote plays, among which were tragedies on Classical themes, such as *Antigone* and *Cleopatra*. He was best-known for his translation of Lucan's *Bellum Civile* (1626–1627).
— *Selwin*: likely to be *Selwyn*, but it is unclear which particular Selwyn is being referred to.
— *Waller*: Edmund Waller (1606–1687), poet and politician, who managed to stay – mostly – on the right side of both regimes. He was regarded in the 18th and 19th centuries as one of the most significant poets of the 17th century, but his reputation has declined somewhat since. He is still remembered for the much-anthologised lyric poem, 'Go, lovely rose'.
— *Berkeleys*: John Berkeley, first Baron Berkeley of Stratton, (d.1678), and Sir William Berkeley (d.1677).
— *Jack Vaughan*: Sir John Vaughan (1603–1674), lawyer and MP. Close friend of John Selden (see above).
— *Porter*: Endymion Porter (1587–1644), diplomat and patron of a number of poets, among them Herrick and Davenant.
— *good old Ben* = Ben Jonson, who died in 1637 about the time that this poem was written.
— *Workes*: Ben Jonson famously arranged the publication of his own writings in several folio volumes, under the title *Workes of Beniamine Jonson* (1616); this at a time when gentlemen tended not to publish their work at all, considering it somewhat vulgar to do so.
— *new Inne*: refers to Jonson's play *The New Inn*, which was one of his biggest failures, not even reaching the end of its own first performance.
— *silent Woman*: a comedy by Jonson titled *Epicœne, or The Silent Woman*, first performed in 1609.

— *The Fox*: i.e. *Volpone*, a comedy by Jonson first performed in 1606.
— *The Alchymist*: play by Jonson first performed in 1610.
— *Tom Carew*: Thomas Carew (1594/5–1640), friend of Suckling. His *Collected Poems* are also available in this series of Shearsman Classics.
— *Will Davenant*: Sir William Davenant (1606–1668)—see also note to p.41 above. Davenant famously had suffered from syphilis (hence "the clap" here) which disfigured his nose.
— *Toby Mathew*: (see also note to p.61); Mathew had written a 'Character of the Most Excellent Lady, Lucy, Countess of Carlisle', which seems to have been taken as an unnecessary encomium by Suckling, whose opinion of the said Lady was more than a little negative (see the poem on pp.31–32 above).
— *Wat Montague*: authored *The Shpeherd's Paradise*, performed before the King by the Queen and her Maids of Honour on 8 January 1633. The play was only printed in 1659.
— *Murrey*: possibly William Murray, later Earl of Dysart, referred to by Suckling in one of his extant letters.
— *Faulkland*: Lucius Cary, second Viscount Falkland (1610?–1643).
— *Godolphin*: Sidney Godolphin (1610–1643), Cornish poet, killed on Dartmoor during a battle with Parliamentary troops.

p.82 *Lord Lepington*: Henry Carey, Lord Lepington, later second Earl of Monmouth, was married to Suckling's cousin, Martha Cranfield. The translation mentioned was published first in 1637; a second edition published the following year was accompanied by commendatory verses which included the poem by Suckling printed here, as well as others by Carew, Davenant and Townshend, *et al.*
— *Malvezzi*: Virgilio Malvezzi (1595–1654) was an Italian historian and essayist, soldier and diplomat, who became court historian to Philip IV of Spain. He went to England in 1640 as part of a Spanish Embassy that sought to prevent the marriage of Mary Stuart to William II of Orange. His patron in Spain was the Duke of Olivares, in whose household Endymion Porter—a significant figure in artistic and political circles during the Caroline era—was raised. The Italian edition of *Il Romulo* dates from 1629, and *Il Tarquinio Superbo* from 1632.
— *Lucrece*: Lucretia (d. 510 BC), who, according to legend, was abducted and raped by Sextus Tarquinius, son of King Lucius

Tarquinius Superbus, the seventh and final King of Rome. The subsequent scandal led to the downfall of the Roman monarchy.

p.84 *Madagascar*. The Davenant poem was published in 1637, upon his appointment as poet laureate. It is a fanciful work, imagining the conquest of Madagascar by Prince Rupert, nephew to Charles I.

p.86 *A Ballade*: possibly written for the wedding of John Lord Lovelace in 1638.
— *Roger, George, Vincent*: generic names
— *Whitson-ale*: beer drunk at Whitsuntide festivals.
— *Dick*: probably the poet Richard Lovelace.
— *Bridget & Nell*: again, generic names, here for country lasses.
— Stanza 20, last line: *Good b'w'y* = "God be with you" or, colloquially, "Good-bye", a word which derives from "God be with you"

p.91 *King* = Charles I. Probably written to be sung to the King on 1 January 1641.

p.93 *Lord Brohall* was Roger Boyle, Baron Broghill (presumably pronounced BRO'ul), youngest son of the first Earl of Cork. He married Lady Margaret Howard on 27 January 1641.

p.95-99. These juvenilia were recovered in the 20th century from manuscripts and were printed at the beginning of the 1971 Oxford edition, which is the source text here. Their first printing occurred in the early 1960s.

www.ingramcontent.com/pod-product-compliance
Lightning Source LLC
Chambersburg PA
CBHW031158160426
43193CB00008B/428